FOLENS PE:

Indoor Games

Chris Coleman

Folens

COPYMASTER

First published 1993 by Folens Limited, Albert House, Apex Business Centre, Boscombe Road, Dunstable, LU5 4RL, England.

ISBN 1 85276402-3

Contents

Den Ball

A ◆ I ◆ M

To move around the gym without being hit by the ball.

RESOURCES

gym or court area
3 large sponge balls
1 box
2 benches
4 cones
stopwatch

Ts

Rs

Rules

Choose three Throwers (**T**).

Mark out an area for each **T** between the two benches.

The other players are Runners (**R**) who stand in line behind the box.

Rs must run around the court without being hit by the ball.

Ts must try to hit **R**s below the waist with the ball.

If hit, **R**s must sit down off court.

Ts cannot throw the ball if they are outside their throwing area.

Rs can rest behind the box for up to 30 seconds before they must run another circuit.

The last three **R**s become the new **T**s.

Progression

The first **R**s out become Ball Collectors for the **T**s.

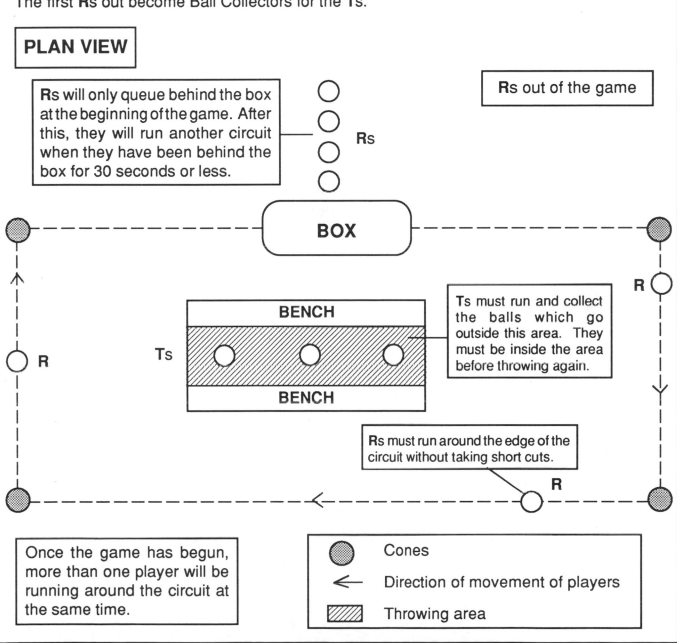

PLAN VIEW

Rs will only queue behind the box at the beginning of the game. After this, they will run another circuit when they have been behind the box for 30 seconds or less.

Rs out of the game

Rs

BOX

Ts must run and collect the balls which go outside this area. They must be inside the area before throwing again.

R

BENCH

Ts

BENCH

R

Rs must run around the edge of the circuit without taking short cuts.

R

Once the game has begun, more than one player will be running around the circuit at the same time.

Cones

Direction of movement of players

Throwing area

Retrieval

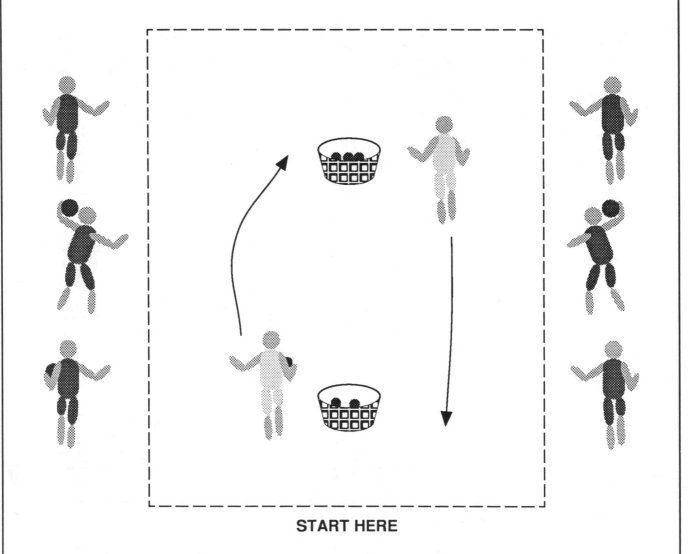

START HERE

Rules

Divide the group into two teams (**A** and **B**).

Team **A** are Runners (**R**) and team **B** are Throwers (**T**).

Ts remain behind the sideline and cannot move on to the court.

Rs stand in a line behind the empty basket.

Rs collect, one at a time, a ball/beanbag from the full basket and take it to the empty basket.

Ts try to hit **R**s with the ball as they pass.

If hit, **R**s must sit down off court and their ball/beanbag does not count.

If successful, **R**s return for a second run.

When all **R**s are out, count their balls/beanbags and swap roles.

The team with the most balls/beanbags in the second basket wins.

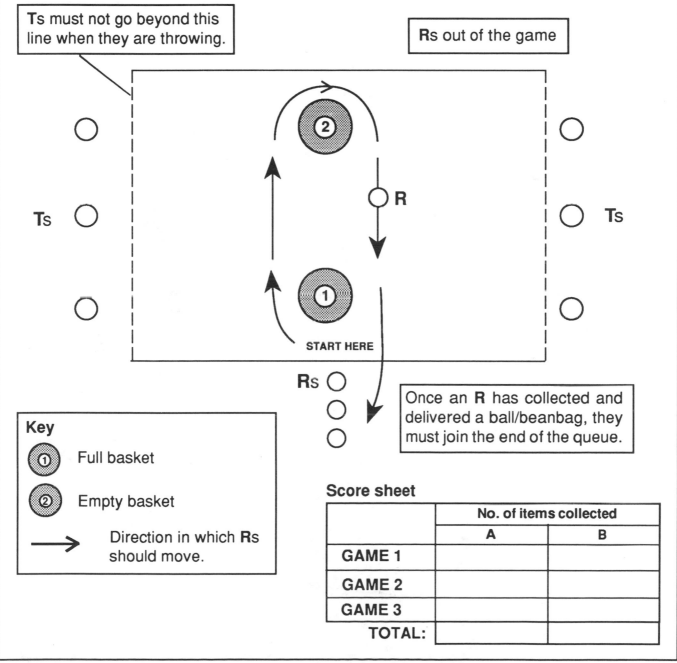

Ts must not go beyond this line when they are throwing.

Rs out of the game

Ts

Ts

R

START HERE

Rs

Once an **R** has collected and delivered a ball/beanbag, they must join the end of the queue.

Key

① Full basket

② Empty basket

→ Direction in which **R**s should move.

Score sheet

	No. of items collected	
	A	B
GAME 1		
GAME 2		
GAME 3		
TOTAL:		

Circle Tag

RESOURCES

gym or court area

Rules

Runners (**R**) stand in a circle in rows of three.

Chaser (**C**) remains outside the circle and is not allowed to run through it.

The first **R** leaves their position and runs to join the back of a new line.

C must try to tag **R**.

When the **R** no longer wants to continue he/she joins the end of one of the queues. The next **R** is the player standing directly in front of him/her.

If tagged, **R** becomes the new **C** and **C** becomes the new **R**.

Rs cannot run around the circle more than twice before changing with a new player.

Progression

When the umpire shouts 'change' **R** becomes **C**.

R and **C** can run either clockwise or anti-clockwise.

Bottle Game

RESOURCES

gym or court area
2 beanbags
1 empty, plastic bottle

Team A

Team B

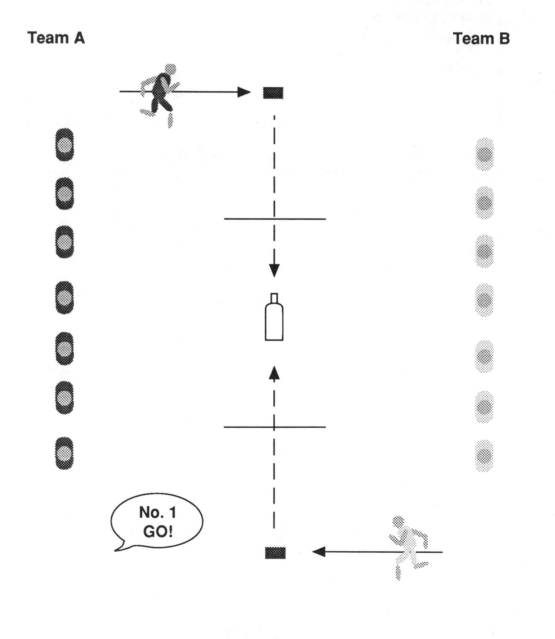

Rules

Find a partner and name each other **A** or **B**.

Each pair is given a number.

All **A**s sit behind the left sideline and **B**s sit behind the right sideline diagonally opposite their partner.

Put the beanbags in the middle of the court, opposite each person.

The umpire calls a number.

When their number is called, **A** and **B** race to their beanbag and try to knock over the bottle.

Players cannot run with the beanbag.

The first player to knock over the bottle wins.

The beanbags and bottle are then replaced and a second number is called.

The team with the most knock-downs wins.

Progression

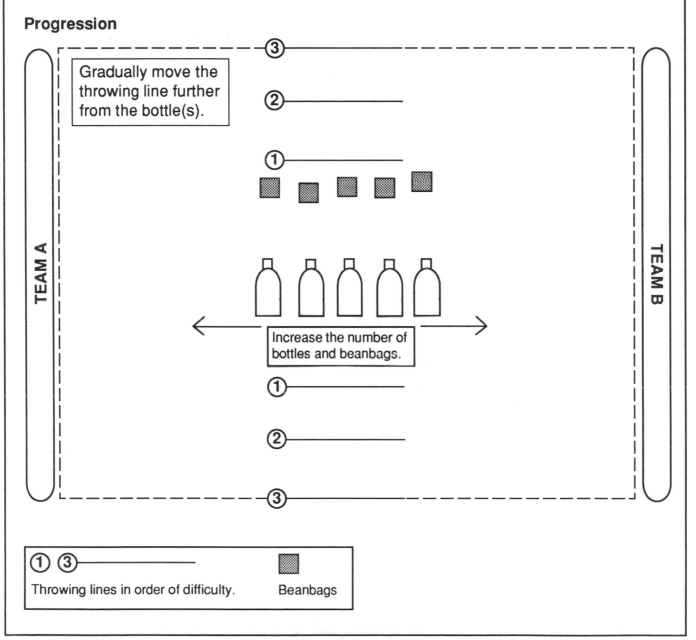

Gradually move the throwing line further from the bottle(s).

Increase the number of bottles and beanbags.

TEAM A

TEAM B

① ③ Throwing lines in order of difficulty.　　Beanbags

Numbers Game

A ◆ I ◆ M

To score a goal against a
row of defenders.

RESOURCES

gym or court area
1 large sponge ball
4 cones

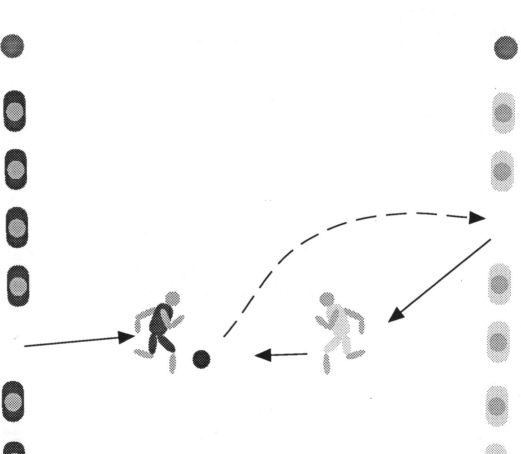

Rules

Find a partner and name each other **A** or **B**.

Each pair is given a number.

All **A**s stand inside left hand goalposts and all **B**s stand inside the right hand goalposts.

The umpire calls a number.

A runs forward with the ball and before **B** tackles, tries to score a goal, by kicking the ball and beating the opposing goalkeepers.

If **A** scores, the team gains a point and a new number is called.

If one of the goalies saves the ball, they throw it to their partner who then tries to score.

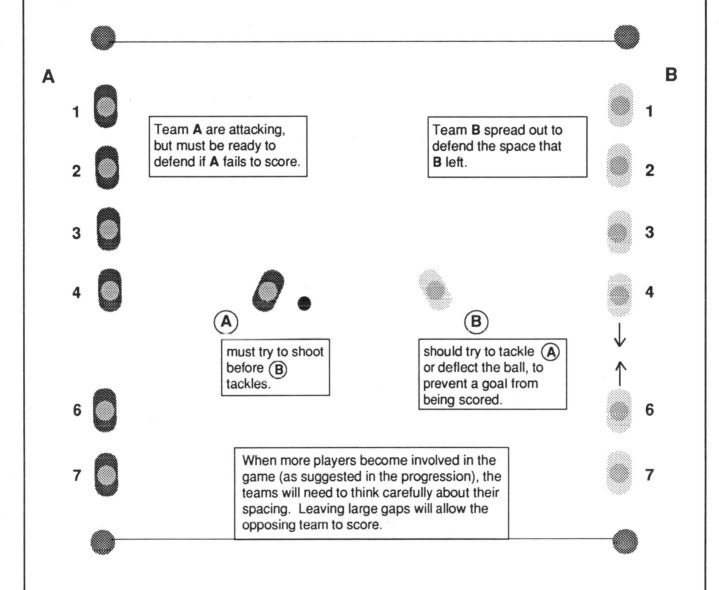

A

1

2

3

4

Team **A** are attacking, but must be ready to defend if **A** fails to score.

(A) must try to shoot before (B) tackles.

6

7

Team **B** spread out to defend the space that **B** left.

(B) should try to tackle (A) or deflect the ball, to prevent a goal from being scored.

When more players become involved in the game (as suggested in the progression), the teams will need to think carefully about their spacing. Leaving large gaps will allow the opposing team to score.

B

1

2

3

4

6

7

Progression

The umpire shouts out two or three numbers to bring more players into the game.

Attacking players can pass the ball between them until they are ready to score.

Allow the ball to be thrown instead of kicked.

Bench Ball

A ◆ I ◆ M

To hit a player of an opposing team with a ball before they hit all your team.

RESOURCES

gym or court area
3 large sponge balls
4 benches

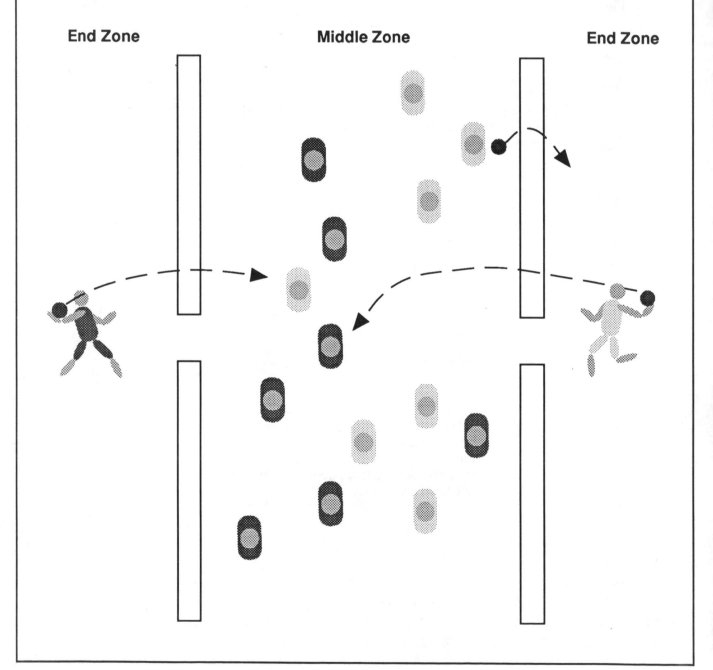

End Zone   Middle Zone   End Zone

Rules

Divide the group into two teams (**A** and **B**).

Mark the court into three zones using the benches.

Choose a Thrower (**T**) for each team.

T starts in their team's End Zone, everyone else starts in the Middle Zone.

T tries to hit a player from the opposing team using the ball.

If hit, a player retreats to their End Zone and becomes another **T**.

Balls that land in the Middle Zone are retrieved by the players and passed to their **T**.

The last team member left in the Middle Zone wins the game for their team.

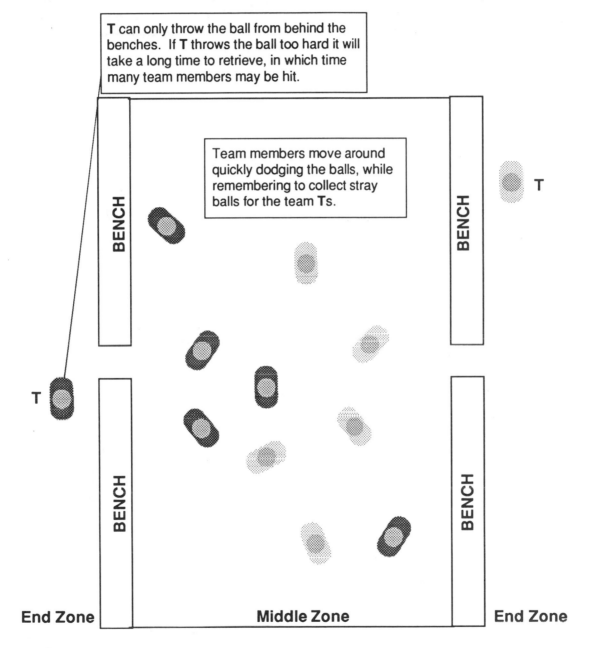

T can only throw the ball from behind the benches. If **T** throws the ball too hard it will take a long time to retrieve, in which time many team members may be hit.

Team members move around quickly dodging the balls, while remembering to collect stray balls for the team **T**s.

End Zone   **Middle Zone**   **End Zone**

Progression

Vary the number of balls used.

Restrict the area the Thrower must target on their opponent, e.g. below the waist, arms only.

Crabs

A ◆ I ◆ M

To keep possession of a ball and remain standing while being chased by crabs.

RESOURCES

gym or court area
4 cones
1 ball for each player

Rules

Mark out a square with the cones.
Choose one player as the starting crab.
The crab must remain on all fours.
Other players collect a ball each.
Players must keep possession of the ball while dribbling it.
The crab tries to take possession of a ball and throw or kick it out of the square.
Any player who loses their ball in this way, or dribbles it out of the square, becomes a crab from the point where their ball left the square.
The last person in possession of their ball wins.

Progression

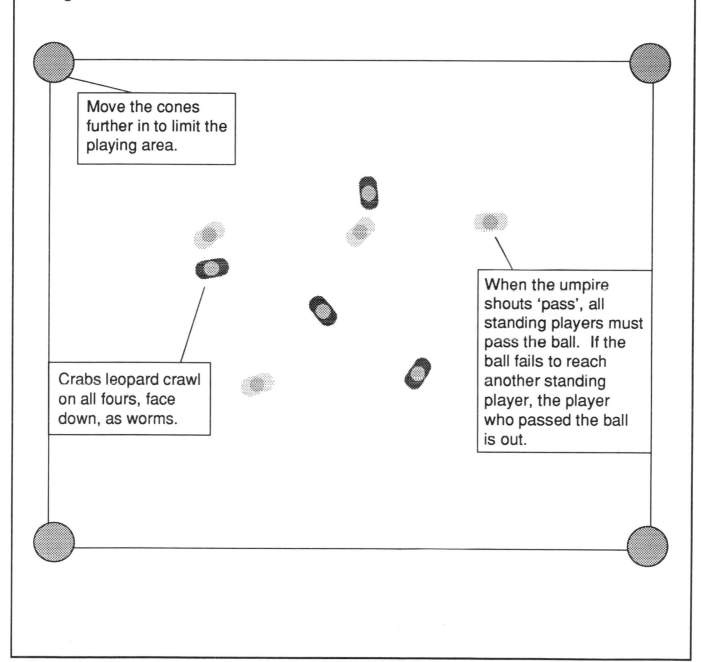

Move the cones further in to limit the playing area.

Crabs leopard crawl on all fours, face down, as worms.

When the umpire shouts 'pass', all standing players must pass the ball. If the ball fails to reach another standing player, the player who passed the ball is out.

Tails

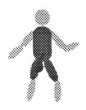

Rules

Mark out the game area.

Each player attaches a cloth band to the back of their shorts like a tail.

The umpire begins the game.

Players must collect other players' 'tails'.

When a player loses their 'tail', they sit down off court.

No body contact is allowed.

The game finishes when only one person remains on court.

The player with the most captured tails is the winner.

Progression

After 3 minutes, all players who are out can rejoin the game.

The winner will be the player to collect the most tails after 10 minutes.

Scoresheet

Player's name	No. of 'tails' collected			
	Game 1	Game 2	Game 3	Total

Crash Mat

A ◆ I ◆ M

To race a player around a
circle and on to a
crash mat.

RESOURCES

gym or court area
1 crash mat

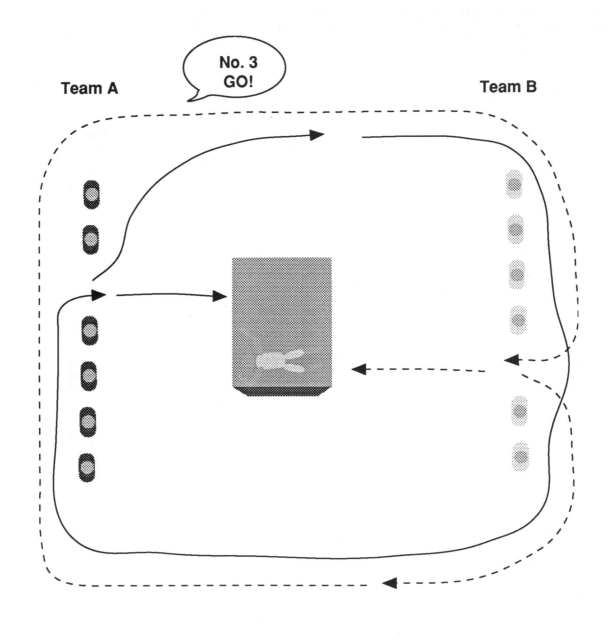

Rules

Find a partner and name each other **A** or **B**.

Each pair is given a number.

All **A**s line up to the left of the crash mat, **B**s to the right.

The umpire calls a number.

Players run clockwise once around the circle.

From their old position, they run and dive on to the crash mat.

The first player to reach the crash mat adds one point to their team total.

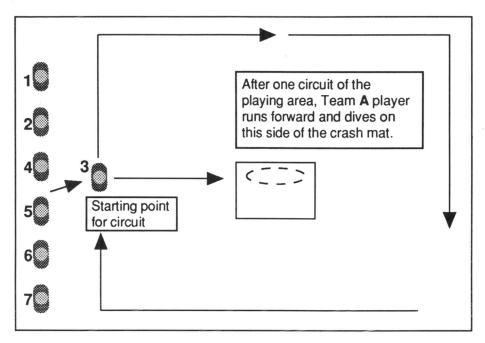

Progression

Players start from different positions, e.g. lying on their backs, on all fours.

The players run anti-clockwise around the circle.

NB: For safety purposes, insist that one team has to land on the right side of the crash mat and the other on the left side.

	No. of points scored	
	A	**B**
Game 1		
Game 2		
Game 3		
Total:		

Long Ball

RESOURCES

gym or court area
1 large sponge ball

Rules

Divide the group into two teams (**A** and **B**).

Team **A** begins batting, **B** fielding.

Batters line up at one end of the court.

Team **B** chooses a Bowler, other players position themselves as Fielders.

The Batter strikes the ball with one hand clenched into a fist.

If the ball is struck, all the Batters run to the opposite side of the court and back to score one run.

Fielders can catch or hit the Batter out.

Fielders cannot run with the ball.

If hit or caught out, players sit down off court.

When all of team **A** are out, change roles.

The team with the most runs wins.

Progression

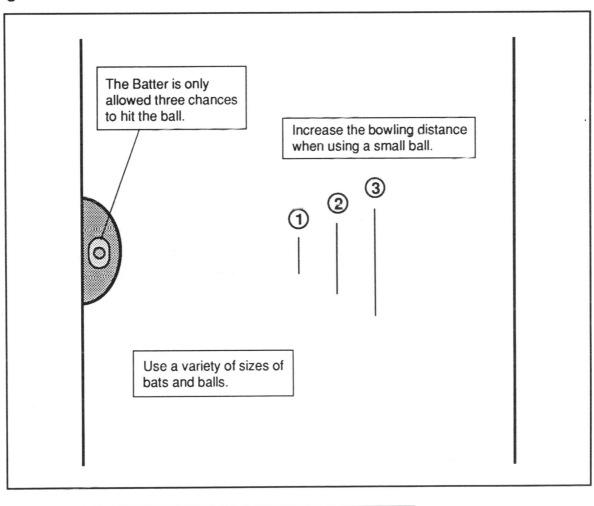

The Batter is only allowed three chances to hit the ball.

Increase the bowling distance when using a small ball.

Use a variety of sizes of bats and balls.

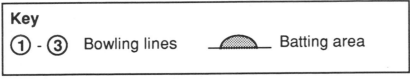

Key

①-③ Bowling lines   Batting area

Alleyways

A ◆ I ◆ M

To catch an opponent who is running through a maze of players.

RESOURCES

gym or court area

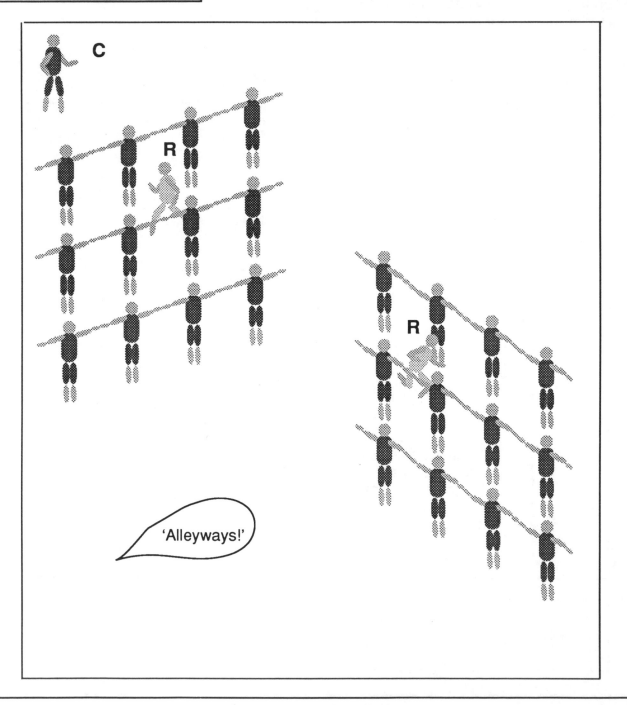

FOLENS PE: *Indoor Games* F4023
© Folens.

Rules

Choose a Runner (**R**) and a Chaser (**C**).
Remaining players stand in lines an arm's length apart and keep both arms held out.
C must try to catch **R**.
If **R** is caught they become the **C** and a new **R** is chosen.
When the umpire shouts 'Alleyways' the players must turn through 90 degrees to form corridors running in the opposite direction.
C and **R** cannot break through any arms and must adapt to the change in direction.

Progression

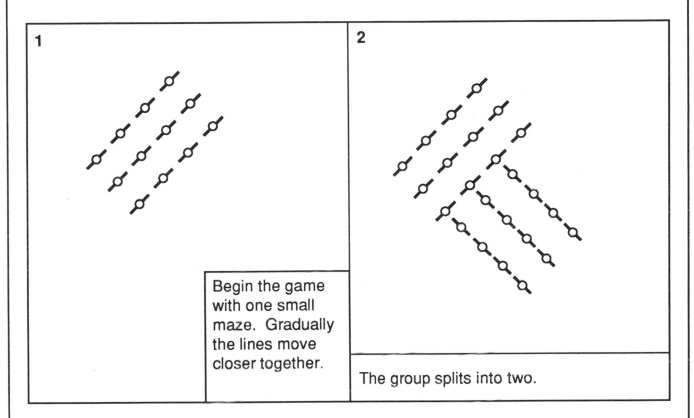

1

Begin the game with one small maze. Gradually the lines move closer together.

2

The group splits into two.

In **1** and **2** the mazes can move.
The umpire shouts instructions to the maze 'move slowly forwards', 'move backwards quickly'.
Choose two chasers.

Keep Ball

A ◆ I ◆ M

To keep possession of a
ball while dribbling around
the court.

RESOURCES

gym or court area
1 ball for each player

FOLENS PE: *Indoor Games* F4023   © Folens.

Rules
Each player finds a space and places the ball at their feet.
Players dribble the ball around the court area.
If a player's ball leaves the court they must sit out of the game.
Players can tackle other players to take them out of the game.
The last player left on court is the winner.

Progression
Two or three players are chosen as Kickers who kick everyone else's balls off court.

Reduce the size of the playing area.

When the umpire shouts 'change', all players must attempt to dribble around one of the obstacles. If they lose control of the ball or it goes outside the playing area they are out.

Key
⬤ Cones

▨ Mat

⟶ Direction of movement

Tally Ho!

A ◆ I ◆ M

The chasers try to put all the Runners into prison.

RESOURCES

gym or court area
6 cones
stopwatch

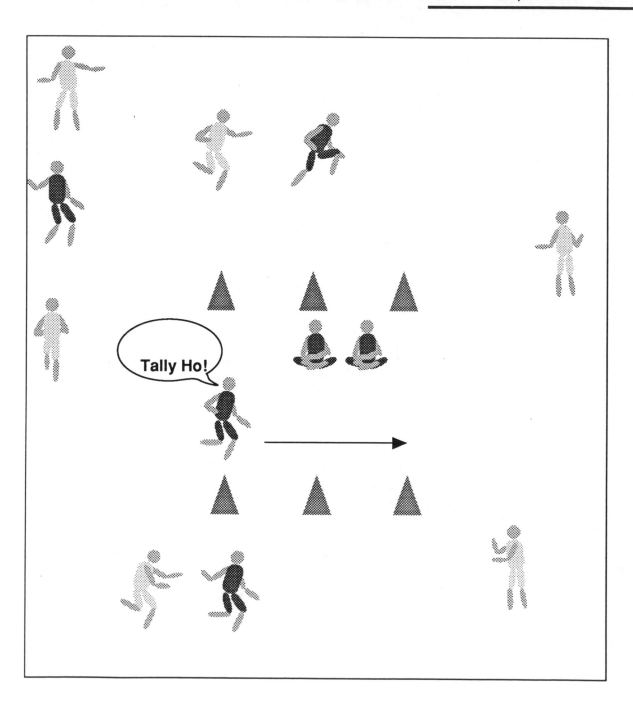

Rules

Divide the group into two teams (**A** and **B**).

Team **A** are Runners (**R**) and team **B** are Chasers (**C**).

Mark out a prison area with the cones.

The umpire begins the game and **C**s must try to tag **R**s.

If tagged, **R**s sit inside the prison.

Rs can run through the prison, from either side, shouting 'Tally Ho' to free all the players in the prison.

When all of team **A** are inside the prison, reverse roles.

Progression

Time how long each team takes to put all their opponents in prison.

	Time taken to put opposing team in prison	
	A	B
Game 1		
Game 2		
Game 3		
Game 4		
Total Time:		

Dodgems

A ◆ I ◆ M

To hop from one side of the court to the other without losing your balance, even when tackled.

RESOURCES

gym or court area

FOLENS PE: *Indoor Games* F4023
© Folens.

Rules

Players line up at one end of the court.

Choose a Chaser (**C**).

C stands in the middle of the court.

Players hop across the court on one leg with their arms folded.

The aim is to reach the other side of the court dodging **C**.

C must try to barge players crossing the court, causing them to lose balance.

Fallen players must line up in the middle of the court as new **C**s.

The game continues with players crossing back and forth until there is only one player left.

The last player caught wins.

Progression

Players run instead of hopping and if caught they have to be lifted clear of the ground by **C**s.

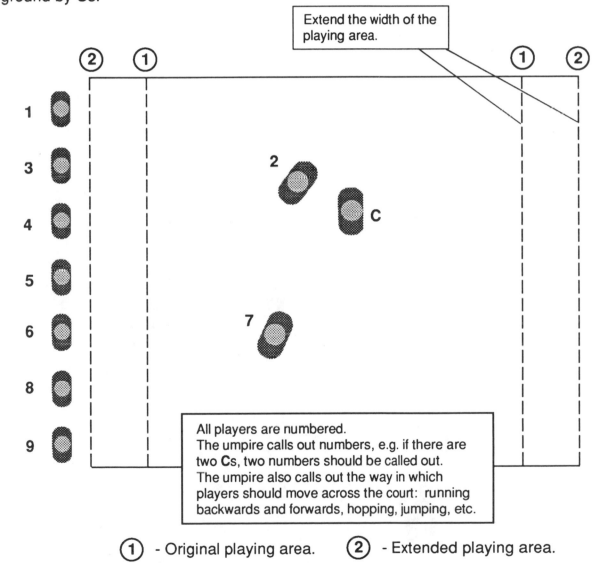

Extend the width of the playing area.

All players are numbered.
The umpire calls out numbers, e.g. if there are two **C**s, two numbers should be called out.
The umpire also calls out the way in which players should move across the court: running backwards and forwards, hopping, jumping, etc.

(1) - Original playing area.   (2) - Extended playing area.

NB: For safety purposes it must be stressed that, once lifted off the ground, a player is set back on their feet before the game can continue.

Train Tag

<table>
<tr><td>

A ◆ I ◆ M

To avoid being tagged and having to join a train.

</td><td>

RESOURCES

gym or court area

</td></tr>
</table>

Rules

Choose a Catcher (**C**).

Players must remain inside the court.

C tries to tag another player.

A tagged player joins on to **C**, holding their waist with both hands.

C is the train's engine, the next player the fender and a third the guard's wagon.

The train continues tagging other players.

The fourth player tagged becomes another engine and tries to form their own train.

A train can only tag if all the carriages are joined.

Progression

Players being chased may rest here for 30 seconds.

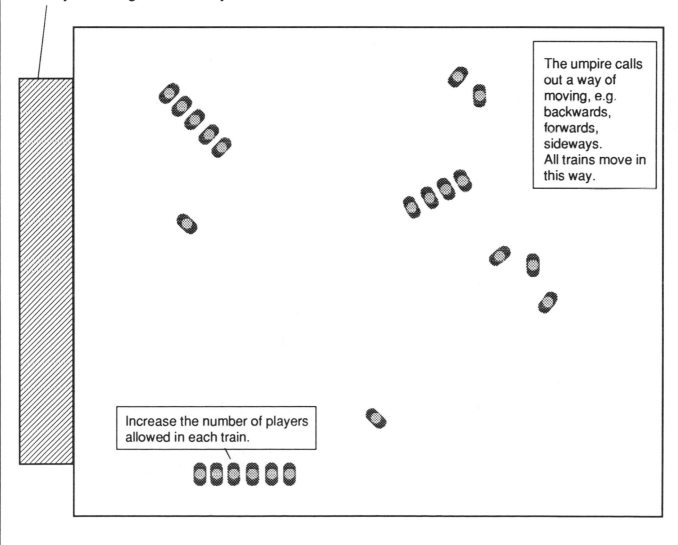

The umpire calls out a way of moving, e.g. backwards, forwards, sideways.
All trains move in this way.

Increase the number of players allowed in each train.

Stick in the Mud

RESOURCES

gym or court area
coloured bands

Rules

Choose three Chasers (**C**) who each wear a band.

Cs must tag the other players.

When a player is caught, they must stand with legs astride and arms stuck out horizontally.

Another player may crawl through their open legs to free them.

The last three players to be caught become new **C**s.

Progression

	Type of movement	
	Chasers:	**Players:**
Game 2	hop.	take double footed bunny jumps.
Game 3	move on all fours in a crab position.	leopard crawl (lie flat and pull themselves along on their elbows).

	Caught players must:
Game 2	stand in a line with one outstretched arm touching a wall.
Game 3	form a bridge on all fours that players leopard crawling can move through.

Opposites

A ◆ I ◆ M

Players must do the opposite to the umpire's instruction.

RESOURCES

gym or court area
1 large sponge ball

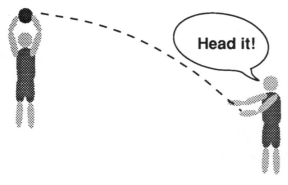

Head it!

Rules

Players stand in a circle around the umpire.

The umpire has control of the ball.

The umpire throws the ball.

When the umpire shouts catch it players head the ball instead and vice versa.

If a player makes a mistake they must sit out of the game.

The last player left standing is the winner.

Progression

Players jog round in a large circle and when the umpire shouts 'jump up' they sit down and vice versa.

The game is further complicated by the umpire shouting 'touch left' and instead, players touch the ground with their right hand.

When players make a mistake they remain in the game but must do six sit-ups.

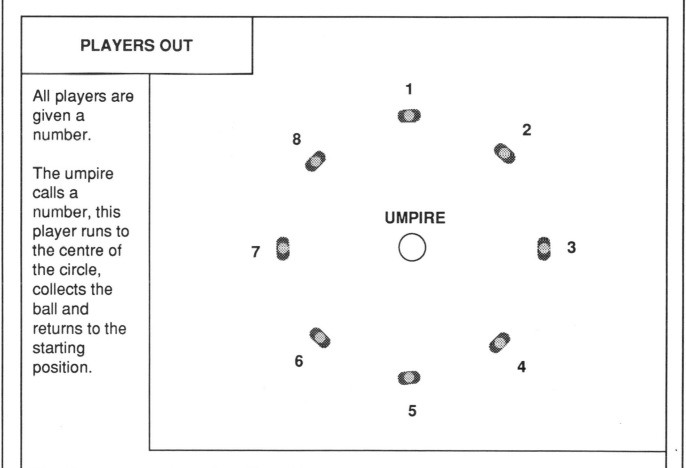

PLAYERS OUT

All players are given a number.

The umpire calls a number, this player runs to the centre of the circle, collects the ball and returns to the starting position.

UMPIRE

The player passes the ball to either side.

Players must try to keep the ball aloft for a whole circuit using any parts of their body.

If the ball hits the floor the player whose number was called must perform a forfeit, e.g. run two circuits.

Fox and Hounds

A ◆ I ◆ M

Chase or escape from a partner.

RESOURCES

gym or court area

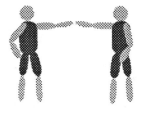

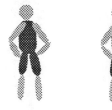

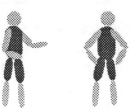

Rules

Find a partner and form two lines an arm's length away from each other.

The left line are the Foxes, the right line are the Hounds.

The umpire shouts either 'Hounds' or 'Foxes'.

Whoever is called must turn and try to touch their side of the court before they are tagged by their partnering Fox/Hound.

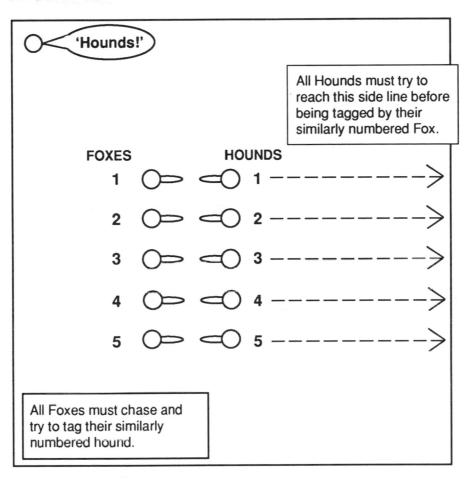

A player scores one point if they reach their side without being tagged and one point if they tag their partner.

Progression

One partner lines up at the end of the court, facing outwards with their hands clasped behind their back; the other partner must quietly approach them and lightly touch their hands. They must then run to the other side of the court without being tagged by their chasing partner.

Continuous Cricket

A ◆ I ◆ M

To score runs as a team.

RESOURCES

gym or court area
1 spring board for a wicket
1 bat
1 ball
2 cones
an obstacle, e.g. a box

B

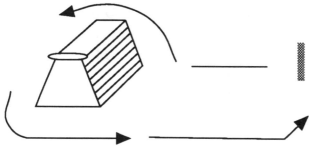

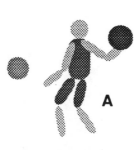

B

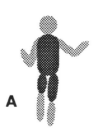

A

A

A

A

Rules

Divide the group into two teams (**A** and **B**).

Team **A** are Fielders and team **B** are Batters.

Mark out the court with a batting cone, a bowling cone, a wicket and an obstacle.

The Bowler bowls underarm and the Batter runs whether they hit the ball or not.

The Batter must run over the obstacle and return to the wicket before the Bowler bowls again.

Batters can be caught or fielded out.

The game is continuous and the Bowler bowls as soon as the ball is returned.

When all of the batting side are out, reverse roles.

Progression

Vary the shape of the bat and the size of the ball.

Vary the size of the wicket.

Vary the obstacle.

	No. of runs scored	
	A	**B**
Game 1		
Game 2		
Game 3		
Game 4		
Game 5		
Total scored:		

Tackle

RESOURCES

gym or court area
4 cones
1 football between 2

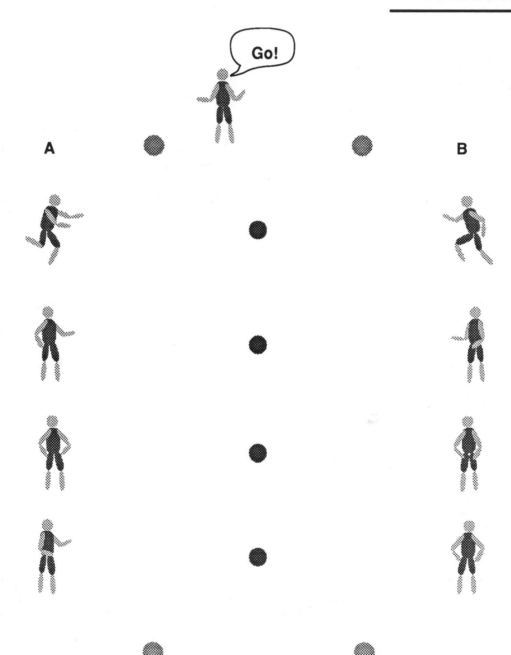

Rules

Divide the group into two teams (**A** and **B**).

Position the cones at each end of the court to make two goal areas.

Line up the footballs in the middle of the court.

Team **A** stands on the left sideline, team **B** on the right.

The umpire starts play and both teams sprint into the middle to gain control of a ball.

Successful players dribble the ball through their goal and back to their starting position.

The opposition tries to prevent a winning dribble by challenging and tackling.

Once the ball has passed through the goal the opponent can no longer tackle.

The team with the most goals wins.

Progression

Teams begin from different positions, e.g. facing the other way in the press-up position, lying on their backs.

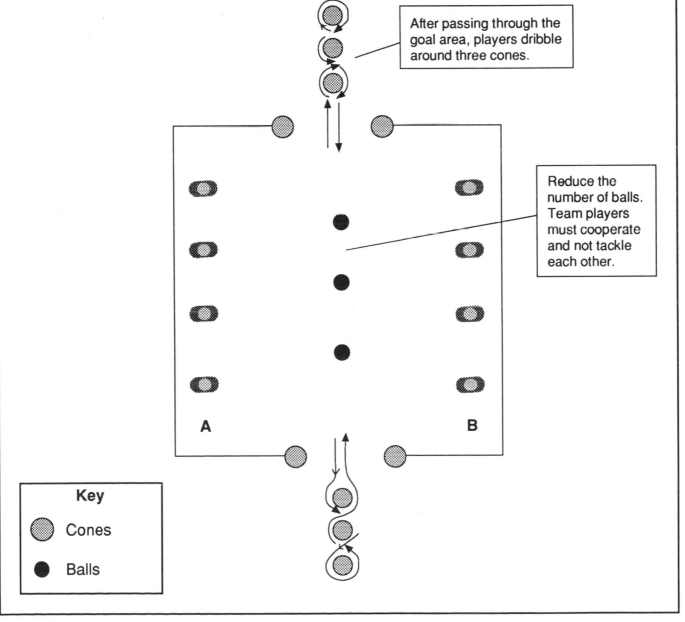

After passing through the goal area, players dribble around three cones.

Reduce the number of balls. Team players must cooperate and not tackle each other.

Key

Cones

Balls

Skittle Ball

RESOURCES
gym or court area
8 skittles
2 hoops
1 large sponge ball

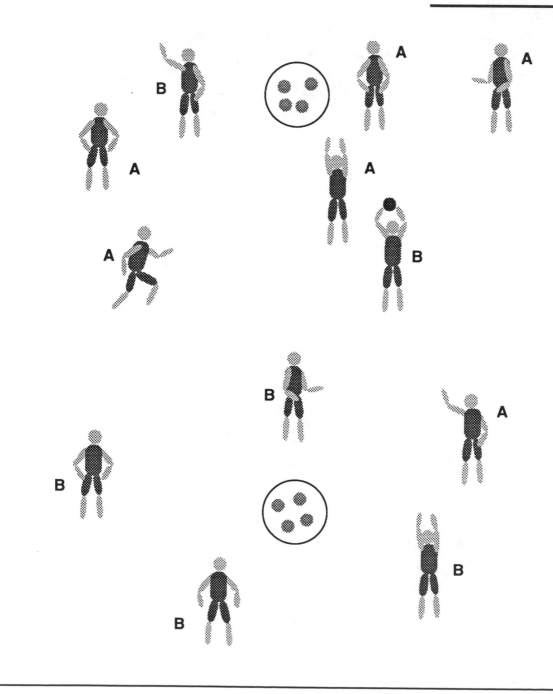

FOLENS PE: *Indoor Games* F4023
© Folens.

Rules
Divide the group into two teams (**A** and **B**).
Each team defends a hoop containing four skittles.
No player is allowed inside the hoop.
The aim is to reach the opponent's hoop and knock over the skittles.
The umpire starts play with a 'jump-ball' (two opposing players jump up to try to catch or flick a ball thrown up for them).
Players can either pass the ball or run with it.
Players lose possession if tagged by the opposition.
One point is scored for every skittle knocked over.
The game is paused while the skittles are placed upright and re-started with a jump-ball.
The team that scores the most points wins.

	No. of skittles knocked down	
	A	**B**
Game 1		
Game 2		
Game 3		
Game 4		
Game 5		
Total scored:		

FOLENS PE: *Indoor Games* F4023

Shoot Out

A ◆ I ◆ M

To score goals against an opposing team.

A

B

**End
Zone**

**Middle
Zone**

**End
Zone**

Rules

Divide the group into two teams (**A** and **B**).

Mark out a team area using the cones.

Team **A** starts with all the balls in their zone.

They must kick the balls through their opponent's End Zone to reach the other side.

Team **B** must stop the balls using any part of the body except the arms.

If they stop a ball they must kick it back through **A**s zone.

If a ball stops in the Middle Zone the umpire chooses a player to retrieve it.

When all the balls have been kicked through the End Zones they are counted.

Reverse the teams' roles.

The team who has scored the most wins.

Progression

Defending players are allowed to use their hands to stop the balls.

The balls are allowed to bounce off the side walls.

The game is played outdoors.

	No. of goals scored	
	A	**B**
Game 1		
Game 2		
Game 3		
Game 4		
Game 5		
Total scored:		

Eight ways to help

Folens PE copymasters offer busy specialist and non-specialist teachers:
- a bank of ready to use ideas and PE activities
- approaches to ensure that children gain essential basic skills in physical education.

Here are just eight ways to help you make the most of the *Folens PE* series.

1 Use selected pages to introduce basic skills and rules. Make overhead transparencies of the pages. You and your colleagues can now use the idea time and time again.

2 Photocopy and display relevant pages in the sports area for teachers and groups of children to refer to at any time.

3 Use overhead transparencies or photocopied sheets as useful, practical materials for wet-weather sports sessions.

4 Create a shared PE resource. Photocopy on to both sides of the paper. Develop a simple filing system so others can find the relevant sheets and do not duplicate them again.

5 Laminate individual sheets for teachers to take outdoors in all weathers.

6 Make copies of selected sheets, file them in plastic wallets and store in a ring binder. This provides you with an easy to use reference for preparation and planning.

7 Teamwork is an essential part of PE. Laminate and distribute selected sheets to groups of children for supervised games.

8 Progression ideas offer you long term planning opportunities to be used as children become more confident with basic skills.

FOLENS PE: *Indoor Games* F4023